First World War
and Army of Occupation
War Diary
France, Belgium and Germany

27 DIVISION
Divisional Troops
Royal Army Service Corps
Divisional Train (95, 96, 97, 98 Companies ASC)
1 January 1915 - 27 November 1915

WO95/2259/6

The Naval & Military Press Ltd
www.nmarchive.com
Published in association with The National Archives

Published by

The Naval & Military Press Ltd

Unit 10 Ridgewood Industrial Park,

Uckfield, East Sussex,

TN22 5QE England

Tel: +44 (0) 1825 749494

www.naval-military-press.com

www.nmarchive.com

This diary has been reprinted in facsimile from the original. Any imperfections are inevitably reproduced and the quality may fall short of modern type and cartographic standards.

© Crown Copyright
Images reproduced by permission of The National Archives, London, England, 2015.

Contents

Document type	Place/Title	Date From	Date To
Heading	WO95/2259/6		
Heading	27th Division Divl Troops 27th Divl Train A. S. C. Jan-Nov 1915		
Heading	This Was Transferred To LV Divin In December 1915 27th Divisional Train Vol I 1.1-28.2.15 Nov 15		
Heading	War Diary of Col A. Lt. Martin Comd 27 Divisional Train From 1 Jan 1915 To 28 Feb 1915		
War Diary	Arques	01/01/1915	01/01/1915
War Diary	Chocques	02/01/1915	02/01/1915
War Diary	Arques	03/01/1915	07/01/1915
War Diary	Strazeele	08/01/1915	08/01/1915
War Diary	Heksken	09/01/1915	17/01/1915
War Diary	Boeschepe	18/01/1915	28/02/1915
Miscellaneous	Head Quarters, 27th Division Appendix II		
Map	Traffic Control Not To Scale		
Heading	27th Divl Trains Vol III 1-30.4.15		
Heading	War Diary of 27th Divisional Train From April 1st To April 30th 1915 Volume 4		
War Diary		05/04/1915	09/04/1915
War Diary	Busseboom	11/04/1915	26/04/1915
Heading	27th Division 27th Divl Trains Vol IV May 15		
Heading	War Diary of 27th Division Train From May 1st 1915 To May 31st 1915 Volume 5		
War Diary	Busseboom	01/05/1915	06/05/1915
War Diary	Billets On Main	06/05/1915	06/05/1915
War Diary	Reninghelst-Poperinghe	16/05/1915	31/05/1915
Heading	27th Division 27th Divl Train Vol V From 1st To 30th June 1915		
Heading	War Diary of 27th Divisional Train From June 1 To June 30 1915 Volume 5		
War Diary	Croix-Du-Bac	01/06/1915	30/06/1915
Heading	27th Division 27th Divl Train Vol VI July 15		
War Diary	War Diary of 27th Divisional Train From July 1 1915 To July 31 1915 Volume 7		
War Diary	Croix Du Bac	02/07/1915	31/07/1915
Heading	27th Division 27th Divl Train Vol VII August 15		
Heading	War Diary of 27th Divisional Train From August 1 1915 To August 30 1915 Volume 8		
War Diary	Croix-Du-Bac	01/08/1915	31/08/1915
Heading	27th Division 27th Divl Train Vol VIII Sept 15		
Heading	War Diary of 27th Divisional Train From Sept 1 1915 To Sept 30 1915 Volume 8		
War Diary	Croix-Du-Bac	01/09/1915	15/09/1915
War Diary	Merris	16/09/1915	18/09/1915
War Diary	Old Area	19/09/1915	19/09/1915
War Diary	Old Area Merris	19/09/1915	19/09/1915
War Diary	Morcourt Amiens Sheet 12 Map	19/09/1915	19/09/1915
War Diary	Morcourt	19/09/1915	19/09/1915
War Diary	Merris (Old Area)	20/09/1915	20/09/1915
War Diary	Morcourt New Area	20/09/1915	20/09/1915

War Diary	Morcourt	21/09/1915	30/09/1915
Heading	27th Division 27th Divl Train Vol IX Oct 15		
Heading	War Diary of 27th Divisional Train From October 1st 1915 To October 31 1915 Volume 9		
War Diary	Morcourt	01/10/1915	25/10/1915
War Diary	Bovelles	26/10/1915	31/10/1915
Heading	27th Divl Train Nov 1915 Vol X		
Heading	War Diary 27th Divisional Train Volume 10 November 1915		
War Diary	Bovelles	03/11/1915	27/11/1915

W095/2259/6

27TH DIVISION
DIVL TROOPS

27TH DIVL TRAIN A.S.C.
JAN - NOV 1915

95 - 98 Coys ASC

TO 55 DIV

ORIGINAL

(This was transferred to LV Duon
17 December 1915)

121/4557

27th Divisional Train

Vol I. 1.1 — 28.2.15
Nov '15

Confidential

War Diary
of
Lt. Col. A.H. Martin. Comdg 27 Divisional Train.

from 1 Jany 1915 to 28 Feb 1915.

WAR DIARY or INTELLIGENCE SUMMARY

(Erase heading not required.)

Army Form C. 2118.

Hour, Date, Place	Summary of Events and Information	Remarks and references to Appendices
ARQUES. 1 Jan'y 15. 3 p.m.	Proceeded to CHOCQUES with S.S.O. to see Supply arrangements of II Division, under instructions from Div. H.Q. Billeted at H.Q. of II Div. Supply Column.	
CHOCQUES. 2 Jan'y 6 am	Proceeded to Refilling Point. II Div. at LOCON nr BETHUNE. Wagons carried out on a road. Brigades nr. Posts being at intervals of about 200x. Road very bad and frequently was experienced. Groups also went nr. There is Bethune and saw St.Q.M.G. I Div. Visited with him I Div. Train Column Waggon had been allotted to the unit for decreasing a part-portion of his hay ration of peace time. The dumping of peace in this weather useless. Returned to ARQUES.	Very wet. Country quite waterlogged
ARQUES. 3 Jan. noon 5.20 pm	Proceeded to discuss E.O.C. conference at H.Q. with reference to Supply Columns of 87 & 98 Co. Arrangements of Brigades to divisional forward move. Visited N° 97 Co. at AIRE. Head goods fit. 80th Brigade arrived forward with N° 96 Co. O.R.C. from BLARINGHEM. 16 METEREN. Baggage wagons accompanied units, 6 pdrs. Supply wagons and as a possible route available Refilling Point for 80 Bde. at METEREN.	wet
4 Jan.		
5 Jany	81st Brigade moved forward with N° 97 Co. from AIRE. Same arrangements as 80 Brigade. Close office at ARQUES.	wet
6 Jany		
7 Jany 8 am	Left ARQUES with remainder of Train, in N°s 95 & 98 Cos. and proceeded via HAZEBROUCH and BORRE to STRAZEELE. Road very bad owing to rain. Great difficulty in picking up S.A. Train horses. Many very late and had to follow. Billeted STRAZEELE. Storm rest-...? Close in arrived at 3.15. b.m. Billets consider 5 p.m. 50 Bgde.	O.R.

Army Form C. 2118.

No 2.

WAR DIARY
or
INTELLIGENCE SUMMARY
(Erase heading not required.)

Instructions regarding War Diaries and Intelligence. Summaries are contained in F. S. Regs., Part II. and the Staff Manual respectively. Title pages will be prepared in manuscript.

Hour, Date, Place	Summary of Events and Information	Remarks and references to Appendices
STRAZEELE. 8/Jan. 9 a.m. 11 a.m.	Proceeded orig in accordance with Bde Brigade Orders. Arrived BAILLEUL. Scheduled time but wires to prevent any further troops being late. Further delay after leaving BAILLEUL owing to wrong order from Ex Bgde Spencer to	Sleet Storm 10 a.m.
2.15	BOESCHEPE west of ST MEKSKEN. Arrived at MEKSKEN. Buses had wagons drawn in fields 5 officer in other platoons on straw. Refilling Point to	Very cold turns rain
	Division at WESTOUTRE. III Br. R.P. also this Remained in billets. much cheering[?] french Store movement[?]	
MEKSKEN. 9 Jan	with several refilling points through congestion. Refilling	
	Complete about 3.30 pm. Railhead at CAESTRE.	
10 Jan	S. wagons allowed to remain with units. Conveyance to proper control. Many arrived late. It is now that the Refilling	
	Rendezvous. 1 Brigade in Trenches	
	2 " - Support	
	3 " - Reserve	
	4 Divisional Troops including Ambulances	
	Puis control performed by Units conveying equipment. Report	
	REMIER replaces D'HONDT as Fewer Supplier.	
	Wagon parks bad. Entrance opened with top possible[?]	Some cheerless among men
11 a.m.	despite all our mileage. Officer Cooks in horse, to be	
	harness things. Latrines to be dug. Arrangements made	
	whereby S. wagons are now returning to units to units	
	and are parked to Brigade in opening field on the	
	REMINGHELST — MEKSKEN road. Wagons incorrectly marked	Appendix I
	Outgoing wagons too and three small busy little.	

O.A.M.

Army Form C. 2118.

No 3.

WAR DIARY
or
INTELLIGENCE SUMMARY
(Erase heading not required.)

Instructions regarding War Diaries and Intelligence Summaries are contained in F.S. Regs., Part II. and the Staff Manual respectively. Title pages will be prepared in manuscript.

Hour, Date, Place	Summary of Events and Information	Remarks and references to Appendices
HEKSKEN. 12 Jany 1915	Orders from H.Q. to take over roads control during march of Supples. Waggons were handed down to Refilling Point in batches as required. Much time saved in requireing Major K.D. MACKENZIE. S.S.O. Sent to Hospital. Capt H.C. YERBOTRYLE, S.O. Du Transport took over duties of S.S.O. T/Lt. G.H. WILLIAMS 65th on duties apptd. D.R.O. Du Transport vice Capt. P.B. STONER, who S.O. Du Transport.	Sickness increases among A.S.C. units
13 Jany	M.T. 95, 96 & 98. On march to BOESCHEPE. This work was made very difficult from the Transfer along many narrow & hilly roads, wet slippery conditions. Also had Routes to be selected by lights examination. Very much hampered by surrounding ground. Lt P. CARDEN to Hospital.	
14 Jany	Rearrangements for refilling in future arranged for.	
15 Jany	Ground arrival from Govt Reserves motor forge as available in DICKEBUSCH area. This is one S.A.S.C. Equipment being withdrawn. Arrangements made to send 2 forges into Ordnance at DICKEBUSCH. S Officers on sick withdrawal. There is also much sickness among men. Try down towards South of town. Lt Troopes sent to Hospital.	
16 Jany	Lt. J. PHILLIPS sent to Hospital with Asthma.	
17 Jany	to HEKSKEN without. Police Guards on BOESCHEPE and made certain rearrangement as to overcrowding.	

O.H.M

Army Form C. 2118.

No 4

WAR DIARY
or
INTELLIGENCE SUMMARY
(Erase heading not required.)

Instructions regarding War Diaries and Intelligence Summaries are contained in F. S. Regs., Part II. and the Staff Manual respectively. Title pages will be prepared in manuscript.

Hour, Date, Place	Summary of Events and Information	Remarks and references to Appendices
BOESCHEPE. 18 Jany 1915	To Railhead and interviewed Officers of 27 Div Supply Column in accordance with Confidential Letter from D. of T. No 97 Co. remains from BOESBUSCH to HEKSKEN, to relieve completion of transport at the front. All S. wagons packed over night - ready to move to R.P. in morning	Snowstorm in evening
19 Jany	Capt 4 VERSCHOYLE to Hospital. Capt 4 FLETCHER from SO No97Co to S.S.O. 2nd J.H. TAYLOR to S.O. No 97 Co. 3 p.m. Moving of S.O. Officers with S.S.O. 2/Lieut A. BODEN on leave. Also T/W- C.J CAFFREY to S.O. No 97 Co. vice Capt P.B. STONIER sick.	
20 Jany	To Railhead with S.S.O. to acquaint him with duties. H.Q. orders remittances of wagons still incomplete with S.S.O.	
21 Jany	Major G.M. YOUNG from 5 Div reported locally as S.S.O. Prearranged arrangements of S.O. & R.O. resumed in No 97 Co.	
22 Jany	Owing to overcrowding another Barn was taken over for billets of No 97 Co.	
23 Feby	H.Q. order for R.A. to arrow supplies by Brigade and not by Batteries	
24 Jany	1 Hoy Cart - attempt for Divisional Train. Sniping reported at HEKSKEN. Reports concerning to H.Q. Div opinion of clothing billets from a map inspection of the size and condition of the same is unsatisfactory. R.A Batteries in places	
25 Jany	1 Regt 1 Horseworth arrives. R.T.A.H.Q. for Cooks.	

1247 W 3299 200,000 (E) 8/14 J.B.C. & A. Forms/C. 2118/1.

Army Form C. 2118.

No 5.

WAR DIARY
of
INTELLIGENCE SUMMARY
(Erase heading not required.)

Instructions regarding War Diaries and Intelligence Summaries are contained in F.S. Regs., Part II. and the Staff Manual respectively. Title pages will be prepared in manuscript.

Hour, Date, Place	Summary of Events and Information	Remarks and references to Appendices
BOESCHEPE 25 Jany 1915	Reported name & S.O. & O. in Town to HQ & R.O. R.O. orders transport RE to purchase spares to	
26 Jany.	Visited billets. Clean surroundings and improved the general health. Clean ration orders for Brigade in Transport, transport a seven ration orders for Brigade in Transport, transport seems very awkward about. 2/Lt Duppler Scholds, except those required for work remained at HERSCEN Opposed under OC troops in town the area RP.	
27 Jany	2/Lt ROBSEN returned from leave. Regan interpreter (F. Kaspabeli VINGERHOETY) reported for duty.	
28 Jany	Visited Billets. Capt C.E. ALLEN to Hospital. 2/Lieut POWYS-LYBBE took over the command of No 96 Co. All units	
29 Jany 10 a.m.	paraded + Clists examined there is there were any stragglers about; none found.	
30 Jany	Sent in a report to HQ. on the general distribution of the A.S.C units both as regards Supply and transport. These cannot be	
31 Jany.	where and service unsatisfactory. These cannot be viewed to units incomplete and some time elapses before they are available.	Appendix II.

WAR DIARY
or
INTELLIGENCE SUMMARY

(Erase heading not required.)

Army Form C. 2118.

Hour, Date, Place	Summary of Events and Information	Remarks and references to Appendices
BOESCHEPE February 1.	1. WESTOUTRE huts were dilapidated. The huts as also temples in completeness with even a breaking window and the use of paper wagons. Were the Divisional Staff see the absurdity of giving over from care the whole of the Supply and Baggage Sections of the Train be present unsatisfactory conditions must obtain. There can at present be no proper supervision exercised, and the possibility of a breakdown where we were never removed. 2. G. HQ. Res. D.S. Sgt as officers - some time visited billets. 3. Surroundings have been much improved. 4. A series of occurred in BOESCHEPE in afternoon - Many wagons still unwashed later enquiry (via Div. HQ Staff. at 10.30 p.m. came into action re Supply Staff who stuck on through The roof. The roof was fitted with taps, which operated. Place was gutted. The personnel had today undertaken the return men of Div: Ammunition Col. train Supply. Service requirements very primitive.	Very fine day A.M. Morton

WAR DIARY
or
INTELLIGENCE SUMMARY

(Erase heading not required.)

Army Form C. 2118.

No 2. Feb.

Instructions regarding War Diaries and Intelligence Summaries are contained in F.S. Regs., Part II. and the Staff Manual respectively. Title pages will be prepared in manuscript.

Hour, Date, Place	Summary of Events and Information	Remarks and references to Appendices
BOESCHEPE 5 Feby 1915	To G.H.Q. with reference to relievn of Sick Officers left with Maj Cadell reconnecting information	weather v. fine
6.	Reported to Div. H.Q. that the G.O.C. 80 Bde had removed force from DICKEBUSCH to BOESCHEPE without reference to Train H.Q. and that consequently the arrangements approved for Div. Staff were set aside. Veterinary Officer doing duty with 80th Brigade. Remount kitchen of 1/og6 Co examine Sanitary place	wet day
7.	Church of England Chaplain held service here at 8 + 10 a.m.	fine, windy
8.	Arranged with A.R.Q.M.g. re forces at DICKEBUSCH. D.A.D.M.S. inspecting 1st Line Transport Baggage Supply &c	v. wet
	Lagers which are suite with limits.	
	To Refilling Point—	
9. 9 a.m.	To WESTOUTRE & saw D.A.Q.M.G. Explained to him that I could not be responsible for Train Transport unless units were placed under my proper control.	
2 p.m.	do —	
10.	To WARDRECQUES to see the Mayor with reference to Requisition	
11.	Slips reported to H.Q. Div. G.O.C. on having been left unpaid by units when billeted there. O.C. Units had left own horses, their Superintendents & Staffs for purchases & forage + fuel. Mayor away — to see him next Monday 3 p.m. —	fine — G.H.M.

1247 W 3299 200,000 (E) 8/14 J.B.C. & A. Forms/C. 2118/11.

Army Form C. 2118.

Ferry No 3

WAR DIARY
or
INTELLIGENCE SUMMARY
(Erase heading not required.)

Instructions regarding War Diaries and Intelligence Summaries are contained in F. S. Regs., Part II. and the Staff Manual respectively. Title pages will be prepared in manuscript.

Hour, Date, Place		Summary of Events and Information	Remarks and references to Appendices
BOESCHEPE Feby 1915	12	Letter from D.S.T. G.H.Q. re return of Officers and men from Hospital incapacitated from my front Strica. The drafts of men sent up from Base have to be been inferior material to own men. New Traffic Control map issued by II Army.	Reinforcement Time in afternoon. Appendix III. Fine.
	13	V. wet.	
	14	The following new Officers arrived as posted as below:— T/2 Lieut. C.E. YOUNG to No 95 Co T/2 Lieut. A.D. DAVIES } to No 96 Co. T/2 Lieut. J.J. HOLLAND T/2 Lieut. C.A.P. O'REILLY to No 98 Co. All these Officers are new & inexperienced & poor A.S.C. 28 Army loads. An every poor substitute for my own Officers. To WARDRECQUES. Now Major. Inspector Regl Shield as belongs to 1st Lancers Regt. There were also others superintending the Division. There was no opportunity this present Commandant have been made at the time of Inspection.	OKM/

WAR DIARY
or
INTELLIGENCE SUMMARY

(Erase heading not required.)

Army Form C. 2118.

Febry No 4.

Hour, Date, Place	Summary of Events and Information	Remarks and references to Appendices
BOESCHEPE 1916 Febry 15	To Reply Post & HEYKSKEN. To D. HQ. int.t.f: Scheme for forming S. wagons & troops refilling at WESTOUTRE. 17 E.3. wagon annex for Hay Carts, as per surveyed order MG	Very wet snow
16.	7 Lieut. Lt. Leaver left for duty as Ass. S.O. Othouille. 2 Lieut. Q. Bowen posted to Supplies - Rouen.	
16.	P.O. re 986 advise to go to HDRES. Recues to a some Pg wagons maintains ten wheel pairs. Meeting ask Q V Corps 4p.m. re composition of S.A.F.B. 213 (A.S.C.) which form is already in use. new Hay wagon Establishment.	Very fine
17.	Wrote privately to Major Gilis G.HQ. re officers who have gone Sick being replaced by Junior & Newer drivers / M.T. drivers. S.S.O. of S-MT. & H.Q. & Services at BEHINGHELST. 18 P.O. re Troops to go to rail at S.P.Q. DIESEN Convenience. P.O. Bus Troops.	Intermindy
	dispatch office for bake. Major THEASKEN. PENNINGHELST. and RESTOCKE in ponsibility demonstrating from in US area. 17/Lieut Cr. Richardson /oner posted to No 95.0	
19.	Two P.O. Scheme re sewn hundredhalls.	
20	Leaver Order retiring from Sick Leave at Mise. to D.H.Q. No billets. G.O.C. at BOESCHEPE.	O.H.W.

1247 W 3299 200,000 (E) 8/14 J.B.C. & A. Forms/C. 2118/11.

WAR DIARY
or
INTELLIGENCE SUMMARY

(Erase heading not required.)

Army Form C. 2118.

Feby No 5.

Instructions regarding War Diaries and Intelligence Summaries are contained in F.S. Regs., Part II. and the Staff Manual respectively. Title pages will be prepared in manuscript.

Hour, Date, Place	Summary of Events and Information	Remarks and references to Appendices
BOESCHEPE. Feb. 21. 19/5	To STHQ at which schemes to concentrate from the abandoned. Saw Corbourn M.O. who pronounced certain farriers as UNFIT for UNFIT to active with Flyarms. To DICKEBUSCH re forage for farriers who in our area, reports to DHQ.	
22nd	Lieut C.A. CAFFREY on leave to ENGLAND.	
23.	Conference of F.T. from C.o. Army Office to consider a further draft of G.H.Q. instructions re permanent formation. Rejaning re man's interview to come reviewing and have products with TAN Donne. To WESTOUTRE and HERSHEN. Called on Capt. SS Bgde re Transport Jam slack Captain. Units still claim ownership of S.B. wagons.	
24	To STHQ re report on condition of a horse b shotgun, reports or by K.S.L.I. to reports that the horse itself the harness to No. 96 Q on 21st & Nyberlin on 22nd has had injuries which were RAD Jro recent nature. Arrangements made slowly Adjvisor of Brigade Co. will meet with Rail Brigade Atficer Sgn Div. Troops chicmed between NEAGRE and BAILENTE. Arranged with Camp Commandant at DICKEBUSCH re permanent billets for Atfican.	
25	Reported about arrangements to SND.G. in person.	
26	To Refilling Point. To S.H.Q. as previous mentioned also (23 Feb) and discussed matters. To STCELE BUSCH.	O.H.W.

Army Form C. 2118.

WAR DIARY
or
INTELLIGENCE SUMMARY

(Erase heading not required.)

Instructions regarding War Diaries and Intelligence Summaries are contained in F. S. Regs., Part II. and the Staff Manual respectively. Title pages will be prepared in manuscript.

Hour, Date, Place	Summary of Events and Information	Remarks and references to Appendices
BOESCHEPE. Feby. 27. 1916	Visited Ributs. General Week of Flint - good.	
28.	Supply wagon of 9th A. & S. Highlanders came in. Horses good. To Refilling Point at WESTOUTRE. To STRAZEELE in the afternoon. Purchase Straw at HAZEBROUCK. Hunts A.H. WILLIAMS and C.A. HUTTON returned to ENGLAND on leave.	
March 1.	Capt. C.E. ALLEN returned from sick leave, and warned Ammunition by T.C. 96 Coy. to CASSEL. Inspect damage done to Brakeing target for which claim is made. (Referred for notice) O.C. Sapper Column. Reported to H.Q. 161st Inft. Divisional and YOUNG wearing no Superintending's Car ordered to return. Train Draft 29 A.S.C. men arrived for various units.	O.A Waiter Col [?]

Appendix II

Head Quarters,
27th Division.

From the experience which has been gained in Transport and Supplies Duties during the time the Division has been stationed here, it would appear that the time has now arrived when a more definite and complete system can be arranged.

Whatever system is adopted the position and accessibility of the Refilling Point must receive first consideration.

In order that the daily issues of Supplies may be made without delay and unnecessary fatigue, it is very important that Supply Details and the Supply Sections of the Train should be in close proximity to the Refilling Point. There does not seem to be any difficulty as regards the Infantry Brigades, and it is suggested that the Head Quarters of Brigade A.S.C. Companies should be near their Brigades. The road HENSKEN - RENINGHELST appears to be without doubt, the most suitable place of concentration. Supply and Requisitioning Officers should remain with their Companies, but should report daily to their Brigade Offices for any instructions as to future requirements.

All orders to these Companies should be issued by the Officer Commanding, Divisional Train. The concentration of the Supply Wagons with the Head Quarters of their Companies will greatly facilitate the proper supervision of the personnel and wagons and horses. Proper repairs could be carried out, and the transport

could be maintained in a mobile and efficient condition.
The Subaltern in charge of this Section would be then
held responsible for the proper and punctual arrival of
the necessary wagons at the Refilling Point, and their
return after issues have been made to the Cook's Wagons.
It may be mentioned that Units do not seem to understand
the difference between a Cook's Wagon and a Supply Wagon,
and they also seem to consider that these wagons are
available for any other purpose. Cook's Wagons should
on no account be sent to Refilling Point. It is on
record that Supply Wagons have been sent to the trenches
and also used for the conveyance of personnel, in
addition to their ordinary duties. The concentration
of the Brigade A.S.C. Companies as suggested above, would
also facilitate the duties of the Supply details who
would be near the Refilling Point and under the direct
supervision of their Supply Officers. Also, the Supply
and Requisitioning Officers would then be in close touch
with the Senior Supply Officer, whereas now they are
scattered, and the issue of orders is rendered very
difficult.

    The Baggage Sections attached to Infantry Brigades
require more supervision, and if possible should be
concentrated either by Units or Brigades. The horses of
the First Line Transport and the Train should be kept
distinct. Units do not appreciate the importance of this,
nor do they recognise that they are rendered immobile if

their Train Transport is inefficient. With regard to the Train Sections of the Divisional Train the matter of concentration presents difficulties owing to the scattered positions of the Units, and the constant changes that take place, but the concentration of Supply Wagons is even more important.

The Supply Wagons should be brought more closely under the supervision of the Officer Commanding, Head Quarter Company of the Train, who could give assistance to Units, and the horses and wagons could be maintained in a more efficient condition. The Divisional Troops are very ignorant of the duties of the Train, and seem to be under the impression, that so long as they draw their supplies, it is immaterial what transport is sent to Refilling Point. It does not appear to be necessary to alter the present position of the Head Quarters of the Head Quarter Company of the Train. If the Supply Wagons of the Divisional Troops could be concentrated at two points convenient to the issue of supplies to the Units, much gain in efficiency would result as they would then come under the direct supervision of the Officer Commanding, Head Quarter Company, and only the proper wagons would be used. At present, they can only be inspected at the Refilling Point.

The above suggestions are based on the present Refilling Points at WESTOUTRE and BOESCHEPE. It will be seen that the scheme, if adopted, would also facilitate the Supply arrangements, should it be necessary to move the Refilling Point, as all A.S.C. Units would be in close touch with the Units of the Division, and the necessary orders could be issued, and confusion as to the position of the next Refilling Point avoided.

APPENDIX III

TRAFFIC CONTROL
Not to Scale.

Motor Lorries →
Other Traffic →
----→ To be used by
Motor lorries when road
is sufficiently repaired

Places shown on map:
- YPRES
- VLAMERTINGHE
- DICKEBUSCH
- OUDERDOM
- MILLE KRUIS
- LA CLYTTE
- KEMMEL
- POPERINGHE
- RENINGHELST
- ZEVECOTEN
- HERSEN
- WESTOUTRE
- LOCRE
- ABEELE
- ABEELE STATION
- BOESCHEPE
- BERTHEN
- ST JANS CAPEL
- GODWAERSVELDE
- BAILLEUL

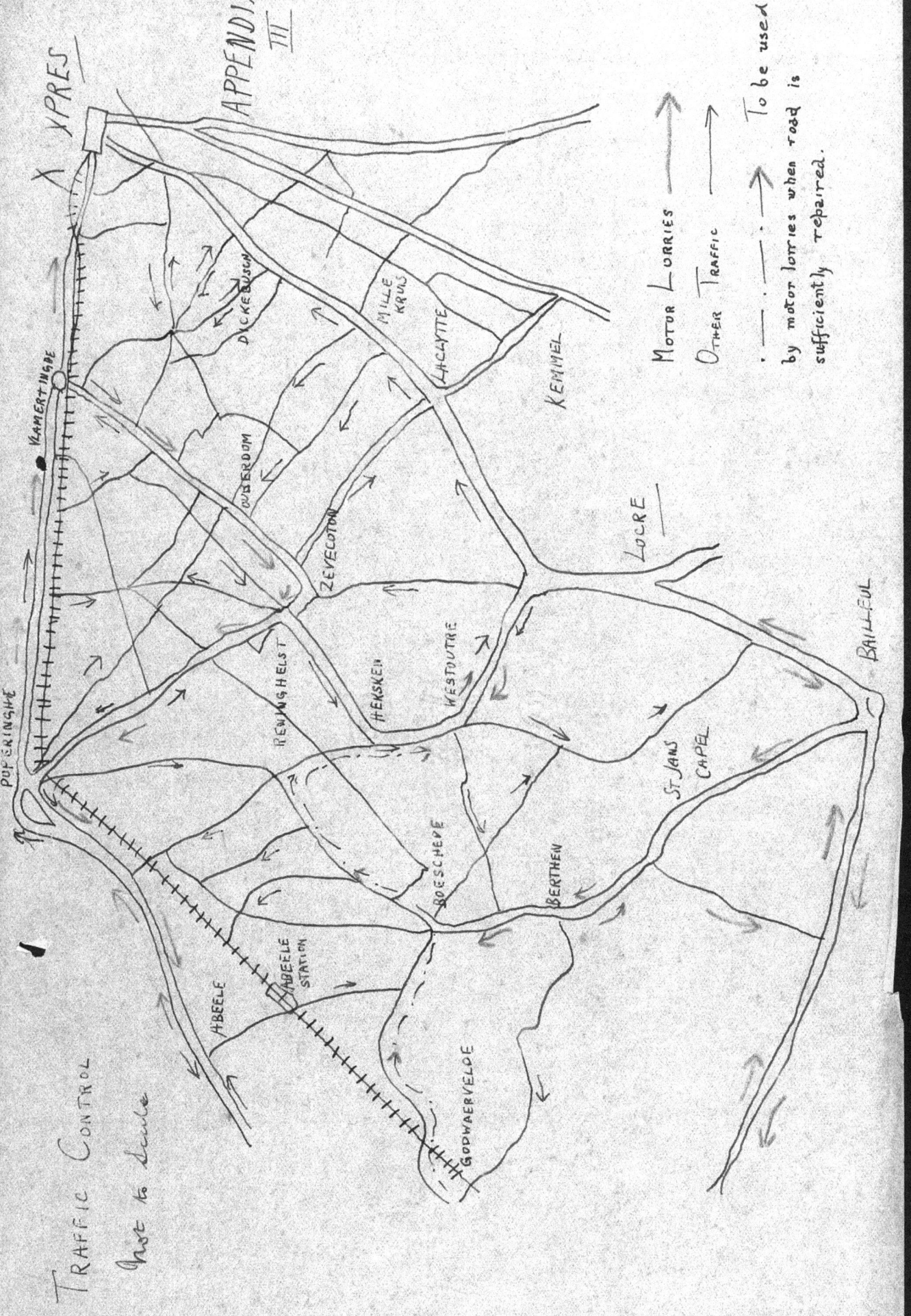

121/5318

27th Div'l Train

1 — 30.4.15.

HEADQUARTERS 27TH DIV. TRAIN
DATE 6/9/150.
No. 2/5/5

Confidential

War Diary

of

27ᵗʰ Divisional Train

from April 1ˢᵗ to April 30ᵗʰ 1915.

Volume 4.

WAR DIARY
or
INTELLIGENCE SUMMARY
(Erase heading not required.)

Army Form C. 2118.

Hour, Date, Place	Summary of Events and Information	Remarks and references to Appendices
April 5th 1915	Concentration of the 4 Companies of train in Billets along the road Poperinghe-Ypres was completed	
April 9th	The whole train (Hqrs & 4 C⁴) went into Billets at BUSSEBOOM. The farms allotted were, in every case, very suitable, having good fields for wagon parks & horse lines. Hqrs of train in a central position in the village. The only difficulty is that the train is about 7½ miles by road from YPRES	

WAR DIARY
or
INTELLIGENCE SUMMARY
(Erase heading not required.)

Army Form C.² 2118.

Hour, Date, Place	Summary of Events and Information	Remarks and references to Appendices
April 9th (cont)	& H½ from VLAMERTINGHE (refilling points for 3 Infantry Brigades & Div. Troops respectively), that any requisition for transport at YPRES involved a long journey of 15 miles (out & home) to perhaps to half an hour's work. However, the fact that Co⁹ are to have all the Baggage Wagons of units with them for a time enables this transport work to be carried out without any undue work for horses, as these need not be worked oftener than once in 12 days & Infantry Battalions refilling at YPRES only have 1 Wagon each day.	

Army Form C. 2118.

WAR DIARY
or
INTELLIGENCE SUMMARY
(Erase heading not required.)

Hour, Date, Place	Summary of Events and Information	Remarks and references to Appendices
April 11th BUSSEBOOM	Inspected Blankets & Baggage Wagons of 82 Brigade which had halted with N to CT rather less than a week. Generally speaking, this transport is fit for the work named, while troops are stationary, but not for hard work continuously for a period of, say, a week or ten days. The Horses & Harness were in fair condition, but most of the collars were too large & hames, in many cases, did not fit the collars. Hardly any Wagons were marked in accordance with the Divisional Order on the subject	

Army Form C. 2118.

WAR DIARY
or
INTELLIGENCE SUMMARY
(Erase heading not required.)

Hour, Date, Place	Summary of Events and Information	Remarks and references to Appendices
April 12th BUSSEBOUM	Inspected Blanket & Baggage Wagons of 81st Brigade. The remarks as to Transport of 82nd Brigade apply almost exactly to 81st Brigade except that the cobands, on the whole, fitted fairly well & very few horses showed lack of proper condition. Harness did not exhibit hardly any signs of wear and was marked in accordance with Divl. Orders (only one correct)	

Army Form C. 2118.

WAR DIARY
or
INTELLIGENCE SUMMARY
(Erase heading not required.)

Hour, Date, Place	Summary of Events and Information	Remarks and references to Appendices
April 16th BUSSEBOOM	Inspected Transport of No 2 Company (80th Brigade). Generally speaking it was fit for a week's trek, though a few of the horses were run down or badly & required special attention which the O.C. Cy and giving. Harness fitted well & was in good condition (a few collars were too large). Wagons in good condition & all wheels recently greased. A few tailboards to be renewed & many wagons required correctly marking. The weather fortnight this transport should be really good.	

WAR DIARY
or
INTELLIGENCE SUMMARY
(Erase heading not required.)

Army Form C. 2118.

Hour, Date, Place	Summary of Events and Information	Remarks and references to Appendices
April 16th BUSSEBOOM	Inspected Baggage Transport of Bdgs. Coy (Batt Trans) There were mule wagons & horses. Variations among these Units were capital, others Horses from some Units were in good condition for work. However in good condition; but some collars did not fit. Wagons, with one or two exceptions, but not many were carefully marked.	[signature]

Army Form C. 2118.

WAR DIARY
or
INTELLIGENCE SUMMARY
(Erase heading not required.)

Instructions regarding War Diaries and Intelligence Summaries are contained in F. S. Regs., Part II. and the Staff Manual respectively. Title pages will be prepared in manuscript.

Hour, Date, Place	Summary of Events and Information	Remarks and references to Appendices
April 24th BUSSEBOOM	The first line transport of the 16 Infantry Battalions having come in from the neighbourhood of YPRES on the previous day & being now brigaded & parked alongside the respective Brigade C.T.s of their rations for all infantry units were located at BUSSEBOOM who 1st line transport & taken to BUSSEBOOM at 5.30 p.m. nightly. This system continued until ⟨...⟩ allotted to our troops. Supply Wagons of trains still continued to carry supplies to Fust Groups as heretofore.	Reginald ⟨...⟩ Major OC 2nd Div Train

Army Form C. 2118.

WAR DIARY
or
INTELLIGENCE SUMMARY
(Erase heading not required.)

Instructions regarding War Diaries and Intelligence Summaries are contained in F.S. Regs., Part II. and the Staff Manual respectively. Title pages will be prepared in manuscript.

Hour, Date, Place	Summary of Events and Information	Remarks and references to Appendices
April 26th 1915 BUSSEBOOM	Lt Colonel A.R. LIDDELL arrived to take over Command 27th Divisional Train.	

2/R Dunoon

27th Divl. Train

Vol IV

May 15 15/5/16

Only 6

HEADQUARTERS 27TH DIV.
DATE 6/6/15
No. CP/33

CONFIDENTIAL

War Diary
of
27th Divisional Train

from MAY 1st 1915 to MAY 31st 1915.

VOLUME 5

WAR DIARY or INTELLIGENCE SUMMARY

Army Form C. 2118.

(Erase heading not required.)

Hour, Date, Place	Summary of Events and Information	Remarks and references to Appendices
BUSSEBOOM May 1st 1915.	The Companies of 27th Division Train moved to new billets adjoining main RENINGHELST — POPERINGHE road: the horses having no further troops of 27th Division moved to neighbourhood of BUSSEBOOM. The same system of refilling continued #75 (refilling was Continued on BUSSEBOOM — POPERINGHE road and no. 1 (field adjoining) Supplies were loaded into supply section of Train and then Vehicles in turn handed as their destination Supplies to 1st line Transport	J.G.C.

Army Form C. 2118.

WAR DIARY
or
INTELLIGENCE SUMMARY

(Erase heading not required.)

Instructions regarding War Diaries and Intelligence Summaries are contained in F. S. Regs., Part II. and the Staff Manual respectively. Title pages will be prepared in manuscript.

Hour, Date, Place	Summary of Events and Information	Remarks and references to Appendices
May 6th 1915. Billets in main REININGHELST – POPERINGHE.	2/Lt. R.B. Porays-Lyttle RSC (No 2 Cy of Train) proceeds to England on leave (rejoined 13/5/15) As hanner weather is approaching G. Routine Orders as to Sanitation are repeated in Train Orders. —	
May 16th 1915.	POPERINGHE placed out of bounds to Troops in VI. Corps Routine order No. 25.	
May 18. 1915.	27th Divisional Train moved into new billets occupying positions as follows:— Headquarters farm M3c 8.5 Reference map sheet 28.	

Headquarters Cy (45Cy ASC) G3id 2.1 sheet 28.

F.L.

Army Form C. 2118.

WAR DIARY
or
INTELLIGENCE SUMMARY

(Erase heading not required.)

Hour, Date, Place	Summary of Events and Information	Remarks and references to Appendices
MAY 18. 1915	96 Coy A.S.C. } L29b 7.9 Sheet 27 96 " " . } 48 Coy A.S.C. G25b 9.9 Sheet 28.	
May 19. 1915	T/Capt H. FLETCHER proceeded on leave (urgent private affairs) to England (returned 27/5/15)	
May 20. 1915	War Office (London Gazette) dated 29/5/15 Notified promotions of following officers of Train (dated 26/3/15. T/2Lt H.M. WRIGHT to be T/Captain T/L'ts C.L. GREEN W. DAY. J.H. TAYLOR R.B. PONYS-LYBBE G.A. MINTER E.S. HARDING to be T/Lieutenant	

WAR DIARY or INTELLIGENCE SUMMARY

(Erase heading not required.)

Army Form C. 2118.

Hour, Date, Place	Summary of Events and Information	Remarks and references to Appendices
May 21. 1915.	T/Lt H. HARRISON A.S.C. proceeded on leave (medical reasons) to England (rejoined 31/5/15).	
	9th Argyll & Sutherland Highlanders (T.F.) 27 Division joined 7th Argyll & Sutherland Highlanders of 4th Division (6 wagons of 27 Div Train & H.Q. horse & 6 drivers were therefore transferred to 4th Divisional Train)	
May 24. 1915.	Notification of an action by the enemy on a large scale developing east of YPRES received from 4th Qn. Div. — all companies warned for eventualities. No known Gas felt with effect as far back as H.Qrs Train at 8.5 (Ref map 28) 7.30 a.m. M 3 c 8.5	

Army Form C. 2118.

WAR DIARY
or
INTELLIGENCE SUMMARY
(Erase heading not required.)

Instructions regarding War Diaries and Intelligence Summaries are contained in F. S. Regs., Part II. and the Staff Manual respectively. Title pages will be prepared in manuscript.

Hour, Date, Place	Summary of Events and Information	Remarks and references to Appendices
25th MAY 1915.	Quiet day.	Very warm & close weather
26 May 1915.	Information received from HQ Qrs Division of transfer of 27th Division to 3rd Corps - No 4 Coy of Train (98 Coy ASC) moved to rear of 82nd Inf Brigade by march route to neighbourhood of LOCRE & bivouacked the night of 26/27th May '15	
27th May 1915.	No. 4 Coy of Train (98 Coy ASC) moved by route march to new billeting area of 27th Division (neighbourhood of ARMENTIERES) & took over billets previously occupied by No. 4 Coy of 6th Div. Train - A 30 c. 5. 2. Reference map sheet 36.	
28th May 1915	Visited 6th Div Train billets with view of seeing Qrs. allocating billets for companies of 27 Div. Train	

1247 W 3299 200,000 (E) 8/14 J.B.C. & A. Forms/C. 2118/11.

Army Form C. 2118.

WAR DIARY
or
INTELLIGENCE SUMMARY
(Erase heading not required.)

Hour, Date, Place	Summary of Events and Information	Remarks and references to Appendices
28 MAY 1915.	No. 3 Coy of 27 Div Train (97 Coy ASC) moved to new Bivot Bde (Sup) to neighbourhood of LOCRE & bivouaced there night of 28/29 May 1915. Supply wagons refilled on morning of 28/5/15 at usual refilling point (near RENINGHELST on the POPERINGHE road) and then proceeded under OC No 3 Coy Train to LOCRE arriving to Battns of Brigade in cuurse at that place	
29 MAY 1915.	No. 3 Coy of 27 Div Train (97 Coy ASC) Continued its move to new area neighbourhood of ARMENTIERES & took over billets of No. 3 Coy 6th Div Train G12 a A.1 reference map sheet 36. Supply wagons of 81st Sup Bde refilled after arriving at new area + issued to unit as usl. T/MAJOR. R.J. COX OC Hd Qrs Coy 27 Div Train committed to Hospital	J.C.

Forms/C. 2118/11.

Army Form C. 2118.

WAR DIARY
or
INTELLIGENCE SUMMARY
(Erase heading not required.)

Hour, Date, Place	Summary of Events and Information	Remarks and references to Appendices
30 May 1915.	Quiet day	Fine bright day very warm.
31 May 1915.	H.Qrs 27 Div Train moved direct to new Divisional area (CROIX-DU-BAC) 1500x over West of Hd. Qrs VI Div Train. (G 6 a 4.5) Hd. Qrs Coy of Train (95 Coy A.S.C.) moved direct to new area took over huts previously occupied by Hd Qrs Coy of 6th Div. Train (H 1 c 1.8) No. 2 Coy 27 Div Train (96 Coy A.S.C.) moved in rear of 80th Infantry Bde to neighbourhood of LOCRE and bivouaced there higher of 3a/31 May.	
June 1.	Supply wagons of the Brigade refilled in same way as 81st Bde.	J.J.C.

Army Form C. 2118.

WAR DIARY
or
INTELLIGENCE SUMMARY
(Erase heading not required.)

Hour, Date, Place	Summary of Events and Information	Remarks and references to Appendices
May 31. 1915.	The Divisional Troops of 27th Division moved in Brigade (R.F.A) as ordered by Divl. Staff to new Divisional Area; in these - isolated cases & baggage wagons accompanied the unit. These moves were carried out on the following dates:- 20th Bde R.F.A. 26/5/15. 1st 19th Bde R.F.A. 30/5/15. 1/6/15 Divl. Yeomanry 30/5/15	F.J.C.

Frank Flack
CAPT. & ADJUTANT,
27th Divisional Train. |

121/6410

27th Division

27th Divl Train
Vol V
From 1st to 30th June 1915.

CONFIDENTIAL

War Diary
of
27th Divisional Train.

from June 1. to June 30. 1915.

Volume 6.5

Army Form C. 2118.

WAR DIARY
or
INTELLIGENCE SUMMARY
(Erase heading not required.)

Instructions regarding War Diaries and Intelligence Summaries are contained in F.S. Regs., Part II. and the Staff Manual respectively. Title pages will be prepared in manuscript.

Hour, Date, Place	Summary of Events and Information	Remarks and references to Appendices
CROIX-DU-BAC June 1st 1915.	1st Apr 27 Dn agreed that S. Sect of Train Wagons (higher) be billeted together near refilling point Bayan. See 1st Apr Staff Company of men remaining in them own billets.	1st warm day
June 2. 1915	Made reconnaissance of area for new billet for V.I sect of Train Camp. Orders issued by Staff denoting water supply in area limited, stating horses must be watered from river LYS.	F.L.

1247 W 3299 200,000 (E) 8/14 J.B.C.&A. Forms/C. 2118/11.

WAR DIARY
or
INTELLIGENCE SUMMARY

Army Form C. 2118.

Hour, Date, Place	Summary of Events and Information	Remarks and references to Appendices
CROIX DU-BAC June 2.	Nothing special to report.	
June 9	Special attention of all companies called to necessity of hiding straw bands round heads of Transport vehicles forming wet water to prevent shrinkage during hot weather.	
June 10.	Special order as to leave for N.C.O's men issued by H.Q. no 27 Dv.	
June 11.	Notification received of S.S.O.'s (A.S.C.) appointment to F.A. Supp. 25th Division.	T/MAJOR E.M. YOUNG
	T/Capt F.T COX A.S.C. took on duties as S.S.O from Adjutant 27 Div Train.	
	Orders issued to division that each man's fray body to contain a pamphlet "Instructions for use of Respirator Smoke helmet".	

F.T.C

WAR DIARY
INTELLIGENCE SUMMARY

Army Form C. 2118.

Hour, Date, Place	Summary of Events and Information	Remarks and references to Appendices
CROIX-DU-BAC. June 14th, 15th.	Nothing to report	
June 15.	T/Lieut H.R. KERR reported for duty A.S.C. posted to 95 Coy A.S.C.	
June 17	T/Capt H.H. RIDDELL reported for duty A.S.C. posted to 96 Coy A.S.C.	
	Special orders issued by D.V. to whole all un-inoculated men to be inoculated owing to approaching warm weather. Enteric is most prevalent.	
June 19.	Inspection of 1st line Transport carried out (80th Infantry Brigade)	

FSL

Army Form C. 2118.

WAR DIARY
or
INTELLIGENCE SUMMARY
(Erase heading not required.)

Instructions regarding War Diaries and Intelligence Summaries are contained in F. S. Regs., Part II. and the Staff Manual respectively. Title pages will be prepared in manuscript.

Hour, Date, Place	Summary of Events and Information	Remarks and references to Appendices
CROIX-DU-BAC		
19th June 1915	Special orders issued by Division as to purchase of supplies by units & procedure to be adopted	
	Inspection carried out of 51st Brigade (but) 1st line Transport	
20 June 1915	Special orders issued by Division to abate fly nuisance	
21 June 1915	Special orders issued by Division regarding folding of Smoke helmets to prevent leaking of eye pieces.	
22 June 1915	Division published orders drawing units attention to saving & prevention of waste in rations.	
	51st Brigade Hqrs. Inspected an 1st line Transport	F.T.C.

1247 W 3299 200,000 (E) 8/14 J.B.C. & A. Forms/C. 2118/11.

WAR DIARY
or
INTELLIGENCE SUMMARY
(Erase heading not required.)

Army Form C. 2118.

Hour, Date, Place	Summary of Events and Information	Remarks and references to Appendices
CROIX-DU-BAC		
26/6/15.	T/Lieut R.S. CARDEN A.S.C. took over command 98 Co. A.S.C. vice T/Capt. M.TUFNELL-KLUG A.S.C. (15 ENGLAND) unfit. 1st line Transport 7/6. 9 st. Field Ambulance	7/6
28/6/15	Visited H.Q. II Army on Conference regarding new Divisional Pack Train for supplies.	
30/6/15.	T4038764 Driver COPAS, R.H. killed by shell fire in ARMENTIERES. Thro' loader of supply wagon P.P.C.L.I. Supply Section of Train Coys all moved into our camp adjoining refilling point (at A 3. B. 7. 9. (reference map sheet 36). This is done with a view to trying the experiment which would be necessary probably on line of march viz. S. secs moving together after refilling	

Forms/C. 2118/11.

Army Form C. 2118.

WAR DIARY
or
INTELLIGENCE SUMMARY

(Erase heading not required.)

Instructions regarding War Diaries and Intelligence Summaries are contained in F.S. Regs., Part II. and the Staff Manual respectively. Title pages will be prepared in manuscript.

Hour, Date, Place	Summary of Events and Information	Remarks and references to Appendices
CROIX-DU-BAC		
28/6/15.	Special Order issued by G.O.C. 27th Division stating his appreciation of the undermentioned distinguished services of T/Capt. C.G. ALLEN A.S.C. T/4/036767 Sergt. DABORN A. T/4/038758 Driver BRISTON E.	Frank T. Lot Major A.S.C. A.A.O. 27 Dn.
30/6/15.	Nothing to report.	

121/6787.

27th Division

27th Divl: Train
Vol VI
July 15

CONFIDENTIAL

War Diary

of

27th BW Armored Train.

from July 1. 1915 to July 31. 1915.

— Volume 7 —

WAR DIARY
or
INTELLIGENCE SUMMARY
(Erase heading not required.)

Army Form C. 2118.

Hour, Date, Place	Summary of Events and Information	Remarks and references to Appendices
CROIX DU BAC July 2. 1915.	Lieut.-Col. A.R. LIDDELL A.S.C granted leave of absence to July 7 to proceed to England. Orders issued by Divl. Staff recommending CRUDE PARAFFIN as a preventative against flies in the trenches – A.S.C provides same from Bases.	
July 6 — 1915.	All Blankets & spare kit bags returned to advanced Horse T. depot at THEROUANNE Proceeding by road — and bivouacking night of 6/7th July at HAZEBROUCK.	J.G.

Army Form C. 2118.

WAR DIARY
or
INTELLIGENCE SUMMARY
(Erase heading not required.)

Instructions regarding War Diaries and Intelligence Summaries are contained in F.S. Regs., Part II. and the Staff Manual respectively. Title pages will be prepared in manuscript.

Hour, Date, Place	Summary of Events and Information	Remarks and references to Appendices
CROIX-DU-BAC July 9. 1915.	Transfer of N.C.O.'s arranged (Issued from Train Headqrs.) amongst Companies of the Train in order to increase efficiency. - The 27th Divl Train was originally a Territorial One & the N.C.O.'s then of each Company drawn from the same district - by transferring some a greater efficiency is obtained.	
July 10. 1915	Visited G.H.Q. Called on A.Q.M.G. A.S.C. & Director of Transport (Item wagons to be regarded as allotted to the Division & not to any particular unit).	J.L.

1247 W 3299 200,000 (E) 8/14 J.B.C. & A.   Forms/C. 2118/11.

Army Form C. 2118.

WAR DIARY
or
INTELLIGENCE SUMMARY

(Erase heading not required.)

Instructions regarding War Diaries and Intelligence Summaries are contained in F. S. Regs., Part II. and the Staff Manual respectively. Title pages will be prepared in manuscript.

Hour, Date, Place	Summary of Events and Information	Remarks and references to Appendices
CROIX-DU-BAC July 14. 1915	Divl. Train moved to new area as follows:— Reference map sheet 36. 1/40,000 Hd Qrs of Train A22 B 1 point 2 95 (HQrs) Coy A.S.C A22 B 1 " 2 96 (No 2) " " A22 D 3 " 2 97 (No 3) " " A28 B 8 " 8 98 (No 4) " " A28 D 3 " 8.	
July 15. 1915	MAJOR-GENERAL T.D. O'SNOW K.C.B. relinquished Command of 27th Division	
July 16. 1915.	T/245 C.A.GRIFFITH A.S.C. reported for duty to 27th Divl Train & was posted to 95. Coy A.S.C.	F.L.

WAR DIARY
or
INTELLIGENCE SUMMARY

(Erase heading not required.)

Army Form C. 2118.

Hour, Date, Place	Summary of Events and Information	Remarks and references to Appendices
CROIX-DU-BAC July 16. 1915.	T/L: R.B. POWYS-LYBBE transferred from 96 to 9's Coy A.S.C. T/L: E.S. HARDING A.S.C. transferred from 9's Coy A.S.C. to 96 Coy A.S.C. (A.S.C.) T/L: H.R. KERR attached to Hd Qrs of Train as acting Adjutant – vice a/Adjutant Capt H. FLETCHER A.S.C. on extended leave due to ill health MAJOR GENERAL G.F. MILNE C.B. D.S.O. assumed command of Division	
July 18. 1915.	27th Division with III M Corps transferred to 1st Army.	

WAR DIARY
or
INTELLIGENCE SUMMARY
(Erase heading not required.)

Army Form C. 2118.

Instructions regarding War Diaries and Intelligence Summaries are contained in F. S. Regs., Part II. and the Staff Manual respectively. Title pages will be prepared in manuscript.

Hour, Date, Place	Summary of Events and Information	Remarks and references to Appendices
CROIX-DU-BAC July 21. 1915	S. Sections & Train moved to new Camp at LA MENEGATE (B19c).	
July 22. 1915.	Rejoining commenced this day (off main road) on the La MENEGATE (B19c) - L'HALLOBEAU (B25c) road reference map sheet 36. Arrangements made to clear farms so far as practicable behind firing line of unbroken or resent straw & restore to owner particularly farm BELASPLANCQUE near BOIS GRENIER.	
July 26. 1915	Railhead from July 26 - 28 incl. at THIENNES. Commenced loading at LA GORGUE on July 29. Inspected Horse transport 8th Field Ambulance.	F.J.G.

1247 W 3299 200,000 (E) 8/14 J.B.C. & A. Forms/C. 2118/11.

Army Form C. 2118.

WAR DIARY
or
INTELLIGENCE SUMMARY
(Erase heading not required.)

Instructions regarding War Diaries and Intelligence Summaries are contained in F. S. Regs., Part II. and the Staff Manual respectively. Title pages will be prepared in manuscript.

Hour, Date, Place	Summary of Events and Information	Remarks and references to Appendices
CROIX-DU-BAC July 30. 1915.	July 29 Inspected horse transport 83rd Field Ambulance H.Qrs Train moved to CROIX-DU-BAC So as to be nearer Divisional Headquarters Visited C.R.E 27 Div to discuss question of horse standings for winter.	
July 31. 1915.	T/Lieut H. R. KERR A.S.C appointed Adjutant 27 Div: Train vice T/Capt: F.T. COX A.S.C (Appointed T/Major June 20. 1915) who relinquished that appointment with effect from July 19. 1915	

121/6757

27th 15 train

27th Div Train
Vol VII
August 15

CONFIDENTIAL.

War Diary
of
27th Divisional Train.

from August 1. 1915 to August 30. 1915.

— Volume 8 —

WAR DIARY
or
INTELLIGENCE SUMMARY
(Erase heading not required.)

Army Form C. 2118.

Hour, Date, Place	Summary of Events and Information	Remarks and references to Appendices

CROIX-DU-BAC
August 1. 1915
	95 Coy (HQrs Coy of Train) A.S.C moved to new billet on A 28 B 9. 3 (reference map sheet 36 1/40,000).
	
	Reallotment of Supply Requisitioning Officers to all Companies carried out as follows:-
	
	H.Qrs Coy (Divl Troops)
	   S.O. T/Capt L.M. BUTT. A.S.C
	   R.O. T/Lt G.A. MINTER A.S.C.
	
	96 Coy A.S.C (80th Brigade)
	   S.O. T/Lt. J. R. ALLEN A.S.C
	   R.O. T/2Lt C. L. RICHARDSON A.S.C.
	
	97 Coy A.S.C (81st Brigade)
	   S.O. T/Lt. J. H. TAYLOR. A.S.C
	   R.O. (not alloted) (2nd Bn)
	
	98 Coy A.S.C
	   S.O. T/Capt P.B. STONER A.S.C
	   R.O. T/Lt W. DAY.
		F.F.C

WAR DIARY
or
INTELLIGENCE SUMMARY
(Erase heading not required.)

Army Form C. 2118.

Hour, Date, Place	Summary of Events and Information	Remarks and references to Appendices
CROIX DU BAC		
August 2, 1915	97 Coy R.A.C. (No. 3 Coy of Train) moved to new area in A 22 D & bounded (references map sheet 36.) 1/40,000.	
August 2, 1915	Supply Secs of Train have had to take up their respective Baggage & Headqrs ? Coys - the scheme has difficulty of working the system of keeping an I. sections of train together necessitating breaking up the formation of 5 companies on S.T.	
August 25, 1915	Scheme adopted by which meat is issued to troops 1 day faster than heretofore has been. In this scheme it is necessary to run two Supply Columns	F. H.

Army Form C. 2118

WAR DIARY
or
INTELLIGENCE SUMMARY
(Erase heading not required.)

Instructions regarding War Diaries and Intelligence Summaries are contained in F.S. Regs., Part II. and the Staff Manual respectively. Title pages will be prepared in manuscript.

Hour, Date, Place	Summary of Events and Information	Remarks and references to Appendices
CROIX-DU-BAC Aug. 5. 1915.	Column in 2 echelons — the groceries forage &c being drawn at railhead for the succeeding days were the Bren meat being drawn at railhead to keeps to returning ford mania to keeps ac once. The new spare lorries thereby parked empty during the day, the groceries forage full. Inspected Horse transport (2nd Field Ambulance.	
Aug. 7. 1915	All Train Companies inspected by D.D.S.T 1st Army.	
Aug 9. 1915		
Aug. 11. 1915.	27 Div. Railhead changed from LAGORGUE to BAC-ST-MAUR.	J.J.C.

Army Form C. 2118.

WAR DIARY
or
INTELLIGENCE SUMMARY

(Erase heading not required.)

Instructions regarding War Diaries and Intelligence Summaries are contained in F. S. Regs., Part II. and the Staff Manual respectively. Title pages will be prepared in manuscript.

Hour, Date, Place	Summary of Events and Information	Remarks and references to Appendices
CROIX-DU-BAC Aug 19. 1915	Inspected 1st line transport 80th Infantry Brigade	
Aug 20. 1915	T/Lt. C.G.I. POIGNAND A.S.C. reported for duty with 27 Div'l Train + is posted to 95 (HQ) Coy A.S.C. T/2Lt. C.A. GRIFFITH A.S.C. relieved as R.O. 81st Bde from 95 Coy A.S.C.	
Aug 23.	Visited D.D.S.T. 1st Army on question affecting supplies + transport. G.H.R.O. 1086 Cleaning supplies - Accounting for pribislios by divisional reserve	J.L.

1247 W 3299 200,000 (E) 8/14 J.-B.C. &A. Forms/C. 2118/11.

WAR DIARY or INTELLIGENCE SUMMARY

Army Form C. 2118.

Hour, Date, Place	Summary of Events and Information	Remarks and references to Appendices
1915 CROIX-DU-BAC Aug 24. 1915	Hughes on all meat from train reported 235lbs shortage to Div HQrs.	
Aug 26. 1915.	96 Cy A.S.C (No 2 Coy of Train) moved to new billets at A22 B.1.2 (Sheet 36. reference map) Inspected 1st line transport 81st Inf. Brigade. 50th Div informed 27th Div that 27th Div Coal store at ARMENTIERES GARE ANNEXE being out of 50th Div Area would have to be moved at end of month.	JFG
Aug 28. 1915	Inspected 1st line transport 82nd Infantry Brigade.	

Army Form C. 2118.

WAR DIARY
or
INTELLIGENCE SUMMARY

(Erase heading not required.)

Instructions regarding War Diaries and Intelligence Summaries are contained in F.S. Regs., Part II. and the Staff Manual respectively. Title pages will be prepared in manuscript.

Hour, Date, Place	Summary of Events and Information	Remarks and references to Appendices
CROIX - DU - BAC		
Aug 30. 1915.	Inspected horse transport 81st F. Ambulance. 27 Div Coal store moved from ARMENTIERES to ERQUINGHEM.	
Aug 31. 1915	Inspected horse transport 82nd F. Ambulance. Visited A.D.S. of 1st Army to discuss new system of accounting as to supplies which renders obsolete A.B. 383.	

Frank T. [signature]
Major A.S.C.
2/ Divisional Train

121/7051

27th Division

27th Divl: Train
Vol VIII
Sept. 15

Confidential

War Diary

of

27th Divisional Train.

from Sept 1. 1915 to Sept 30. 1915.

Volume. 6.

Army Form C. 2118.

WAR DIARY
or
INTELLIGENCE SUMMARY
(Erase heading not required.)

Instructions regarding War Diaries and Intelligence Summaries are contained in F. S. Regs., Part II. and the Staff Manual respectively. Title pages will be prepared in manuscript.

Hour, Date, Place	Summary of Events and Information	Remarks and references to Appendices
CROIX-DU-BAC Sept 1. 1915.	Inspected horse transport - 83rd Field Ambulance. T/Lieut H. HARRISON A.S.C. struck off Strength of Div Train having been invalided to England.	
Sept 3. 1915	Normal system of supplies handed to Divn. Supplies of each commodity [struck through] in supply Column lorries resumed.	
Sept 4. 1915	ATB 383 Supply Officer's many discontinued from this date. The new system of supply accounting commencing on Sept 5. Visited S.S.O's meeting 3rd Corps Headquarters	
Sept 7. 1915	Visited MERRIS H.Qrs 23rd Dn to arrange for attachments of supply details & (transport details) whilst 69th & 70th Inf Brigades are attached to 27 Dn for instruction.	J.76

1247 W 3299 200,000 (E) 8/14 J.B.C. & A. Forms/C. 2118/11.

Army Form C. 2118.

WAR DIARY
or
INTELLIGENCE SUMMARY

(Erase heading not required.)

Instructions regarding War Diaries and Intelligence Summaries are contained in F. S. Regs., Part II. and the Staff Manual respectively. Title pages will be prepared in manuscript.

Hour, Date, Place	Summary of Events and Information	Remarks and references to Appendices
CROIX-DU-BAC		
Sept 8. 1915.		
Sept 9. 1915.	Visited neighbourhood of FLEURBAIX to examine area of proposed system of trench railways for carrying supplies to trench troops in winter.	
Sept 10. 1915. Sept 11. 1915. Sept 13. 1915.	Intimation that these 2 Divs would be withdrawn from area next to a new one. Orders issued for Baggage sections of the Train to accompany units on move by rail of the Division to new area.	
Sept 14. 1915.	83rd Infantry Bde relieved by 70th Inf Bde (23rd Div) – & on relief marched to new area in neighbourhood of GRAND SEC BOIS. 80th Infantry Bde marched to new area in neighbourhood of PRADELLES.	

J.F.G.

Army Form C. 2118.

WAR DIARY
or
INTELLIGENCE SUMMARY
(Erase heading not required.)

Hour, Date, Place	Summary of Events and Information	Remarks and references to Appendices
CROIX-DU-BAC		
Sept 14. 1915.	96 Coy ASC moved to new area (neighbourhood of STRAZELLE. T/Capt. H.M.WRIGHT A.S.C. rejoined Train now entered sick leave.	
Sept 15. 1915.	Supplying wagons of all units who marched to new area on Sept 14 & of those who marched on Sept 15 after refilling in LA MENEGATE - L'HALLOBEAU road at 6.30 am proceeded to new area & after dumping supplies with units reported to 96 & 98 Coy RE already in new area. 98 Coy ASC moved to new area in neighbourhood of GRAND SEC-BOIS Vacated coal store in ERQUINHEM handing over coal in hand to S.S.O. 23 Division	JHG

WAR DIARY or INTELLIGENCE SUMMARY

Army Form C. 2118.

Hour, Date, Place	Summary of Events and Information	Remarks and references to Appendices
MERRIS. Sept. 16. 1915	Hd Qrs. 27 Div Train moved to nineteen (also 95 Coy ASC) billets in and neighbourhood of MERRIS. Div. HQrs moved to MERRIS. Refilling carried out as under :- 81.'s formation & 80th Bde formation at 7.45 a.m. on the road running South from the M in MOOLENACKER. 82nd Bde formation at 8.45 a.m. on road running East from PRADELLES at cross roads just below LL in PRADELLES. 81st Bde formation at 8.45 a.m. on road L'MENEGATE - HALLOYBEAU road.	
HAZEBROUCK 5A map		

Army Form C. 2118.

WAR DIARY
or
INTELLIGENCE SUMMARY
(Erase heading not required.)

Hour, Date, Place	Summary of Events and Information	Remarks and references to Appendices
MERRIS. SEPT 17, 1915	81st Sit Bde - 81st Field Ambulance & } move station 97 Cy A.S.C. moved to rendezvous in } 5.30 a.m. neighbourhood of VIEUX-BERQUIN. Supply wagons of these units proven empty and refilled on main NEUF-BERQUIN - VIEUX BERQUIN road at 9.30 a.m. near LA COURONNE - after refilling proceeded to unit. Thence to 97 Coy A.S.C. All other formations refilled as on Sept 16. Units who entrained on 16th depot for move to 3rd Army area refilled in afternoon with supplies for consumption on Sept 18. These supplies carried free on the Train Journey on 18th Refilling took place on main MOOLENACKE R - MERRIS road.	J.H.

WAR DIARY
or
INTELLIGENCE SUMMARY

(Erase heading not required.)

Army Form C. 2118.

Hour, Date, Place	Summary of Events and Information	Remarks and references to Appendices
MERRIS Sept 17. 1915	T/2 Lt. O. BOULTON joined 27 Div. Train (posted to 96 Coy A.S.C.)	
Sept 18. 1915	27 (Div. Aca.) (Hd. qrs.) arrived at 27 Div railhead BAC - ST. MAUR & then proceeded to new 3rd army area loaded with supplies for those units who entrained on Sept 18. All units (less those who entrained on the day) retired to - on Sept 17. 2nd/3rd Bde formation & portion of Div. Trans. (Div. Trans.) Those units who entrained on 19th Sept. refilled again at 1-30 pm with supplies for consumption Sept 20. These supplies carried in supply wagons by rail journey Sept 19 at HAZEBROUCK. 96 Coy A.S.C. entrained & proceeded to new area.	F.H.

Army Form C. 2118.

WAR DIARY
or
INTELLIGENCE SUMMARY
(Erase heading not required.)

Instructions regarding War Diaries and Intelligence Summaries are contained in F. S. Regs., Part II. and the Staff Manual respectively. Title pages will be prepared in manuscript.

Hour, Date, Place	Summary of Events and Information	Remarks and references to Appendices
MERRIS Sept 18. 1915.	A.M. HdQrs entrained for new area. HdQrs 27 Div Train & 95 Coy A.S.C. entrained at THIENNES proceeded by rail to new area.	
OLD AREA Sept 19. 1915.	27 Div S. Col. (T & S) arrived at 27 Div railhead BAC-ST-MAUR & then proceeded to 3rd Army area loaded with supplies for those units who entrained on Sept 19. Remaining portion of 27 Div in old area refilled as on morning of Sept 18 — in the afternoon units refilled again supplies for Consumption Sept 21. (carried out supply wagon on Rail journey 20th Sept.) 95 Coy A.S.C. entrained at HAZEBROUCK for new Third Army area.	

F.J.C.

1247 W 3299 200,000 (E) 8/14 J.B.C. & A. Forms/C. 2118/11.

WAR DIARY
or
INTELLIGENCE SUMMARY
(Erase heading not required.)

Army Form C. 2118.

Instructions regarding War Diaries and Intelligence Summaries are contained in F. S. Regs., Part II. and the Staff Manual respectively. Title pages will be prepared in manuscript.

Hour, Date, Place	Summary of Events and Information	Remarks and references to Appendices
OLD AREA MERRIS. Sept 19. 1915.	27 Div S.Col loaded at railhead BAC-ST-MAUR remaining portion in afternoon this morning. Sept 20 proceeded to newarea.	
MORCOURT. AMIENS SHEET 12. map. Sept 19. 1915.	27 Div Train Henaghs and 95Coy ASC detrained at GUILLAUCOURT proceeded by road & billeted at MORCOURT. 96 Coy ASC also detrained at GUILLAUCOURT proceeded by road & billeted at CERISY-GAILLY. 27 Div A.Col 1st portion arrived at newarea and was billeted at FOUILLOY. 27 Div S.Col arrived in afternoon at new railhead MARCEL CAVE.	F.J.G

Army Form C. 2118.

WAR DIARY
or
INTELLIGENCE SUMMARY
(Erase heading not required.)

Hour, Date, Place	Summary of Events and Information	Remarks and references to Appendices
MORCOURT Sept 19. 1915.	All units who travelled by train 18th/ arrived at cross roads between LE-HAMEL and CERISY-GAILLY	
MERRIS (old area) Sept. 20. 1915.	97 Coy A.S.C. entrained at HAZEBROUCK. This remainder of Division party at STEENBECQUE reported arrival at THIENNES.	
MORCOURT new area Sept 20. 1915.	had reconnaissance of new area to location of refilling points taken from road traffic point of view. Refilling during day at crossroads LE HAMEL - CERISY GAILLY of all units in area who detrained on Sept 19-20.	98 Coy A.S.C. detrained at GUILLAUCOURT and proceeded to billet at CERISY GAILLY

WAR DIARY
or
INTELLIGENCE SUMMARY

(Erase heading not required.)

Army Form C. 2118.

Hour, Date, Place	Summary of Events and Information	Remarks and references to Appendices
MORCOURT Sept 21. 1915.	Refitting of Division took place during morning to form as follows:- **81st Bde formation** Crossroads between LE HAMEL and CERISY GAILLY. **82nd Bde formation** Square at CERISY - GAILLY **83rd Bde formation** MORCOURT 97th Coy A.S.C. attached to GUILLAUCOURT proceeded to billets at CERISY GAILLY. 2nd Lt. Ch. RICHARDSON posted from R.O. 80th Bde to 97th Coy A.S.C. as Transport subaltern. T/2 Lt. H. DOHERTY A.S.C. posted 27 Div Train posted to 95th Coy A.S.C. Refitting during day at billets at CERISY-GAILLY	J.J.G

Army Form C. 2118.

WAR DIARY
or
INTELLIGENCE SUMMARY

(Erase heading not required.)

Instructions regarding War Diaries and Intelligence Summaries are contained in F. S. Regs., Part II. and the Staff Manual respectively. Title pages will be prepared in manuscript.

Hour, Date, Place	Summary of Events and Information	Remarks and references to Appendices
MORCOURT. SEPT 22.	27 Div Railhead changed to VILLERS BRETONNEUX. Refilling of Division to on Sept. 22. Time 4. 30 am. All wagons (Supply) which had been retained by units for the move of the Division returned after dumping supplies, to their respective companies with loading record parties representative of units.	
Sept 23.	/	
Sept 25.	T/ Lt. E.S. HARDING A.S.C. allotted from Transport establishment 96 Coy A.S.C. to R.O. 80/15. Brigade (96 Coy A.S.C.)	J.I.C.

Army Form C. 2118.

WAR DIARY
or
INTELLIGENCE SUMMARY
(Erase heading not required.)

Hour, Date, Place	Summary of Events and Information	Remarks and references to Appendices
MORCOURT. Sept 26.	Reported for S.S.O's meeting at Corps Headquarters - GLISSY. (near AMIENS.) Visited D.D.S.T. 3rd Army to arrange supply of coal for new area. Refixing of formations as follows:- 80th) Brigade MERICOURT 9am. Bn's) Dis! Troops MORCOURT 9am. Aux Bde formation CERISY GAILLY. 9am. T/L: R.B. POWYS LYBBE A.S.C. allotted from Transport and 95 Coy A.S.C. to Transport and 95 Coy A.S.C. T/JL: CAP. O'REILLY A.S.C. allotted from Transport and 95 Coy A.S.C. to Transport and 95 Coy A.S.C.	F.J.K.

Army Form C. 2118.

WAR DIARY
or
INTELLIGENCE SUMMARY
(Erase heading not required.)

Hour, Date, Place	Summary of Events and Information	Remarks and references to Appendices
MORCOURT Sept 27. 1915	Visited LONG PRÉ to arrange aircraft of coal left by Indian Cavalry Corps to be transferred to 27 Div railhead.	Very well
Sept 28. 1915	Visited Indian Supply Depôt CANAPLES. 81st Bde formation refilems at MORCOURT. All other units as before.	
Sept 29. 1915	Circular memo issued by Division an regards certain actions to be taken in case of forward move. Arranged with S.S.O. 26 Div for a few units attached to 27 Div for training to be refilems in our area.	(27 Div No 2646) F.T.C.

1247 W 3299 200,000 (E) 8/14 J.B.C. & A. Forms/C. 2118/14

Army Form C. 2118.

WAR DIARY
or
INTELLIGENCE SUMMARY
(Erase heading not required.)

Instructions regarding War Diaries and Intelligence Summaries are contained in F. S. Regs., Part II. and the Staff Manual respectively. Title pages will be prepared in manuscript.

Hour, Date, Place	Summary of Events and Information	Remarks and references to Appendices
MORCOURT. Apr 30, 1915	No orders issued by Division. Captain GUILLUCOURT took over coal which had been sent here in error, from LONGPRE.	Frank T. Pye Major ASC A.D.O. 27 Division (27 Divisional Train)

121/7378

27th Division

27th Divl Trains
Vol IX
Oct 15

CONFIDENTIAL

War Diary

of

27th Divisional Train

from October 1st 1915 to October 31. 1915.

Volume 9

WAR DIARY
or
INTELLIGENCE SUMMARY

Army Form C. 2118.

Hour, Date, Place	Summary of Events and Information	Remarks and references to Appendices
MORCOURT. Dec 1. 1915	96 Coy A.S.C. moved from CERISY - GAILLY to LAHEUVILLE - BRAY. Acting under 13th Corps mine R.397 dated 30th Sept. Supplying sections of Train afilesse in afternoon and parked on their own company lines during night. Proceeding to units next morning. Supply Column lorries parked all night empty to this system to be carried out until further orders.	Fine bright All day
Dec 2. 1915	Visits D.D.S.&T. 3rd Army, re drawing of heavier comforts from CHAPLES. Refilling took place as follows 4/pm. B Troops formation MORCOURT 81st Bde formation " 60th Brigade " MERICOURT 62nd " CERISY GAILLY.	J.76

Army Form C. 2118.

WAR DIARY
or
INTELLIGENCE SUMMARY
(Erase heading not required.)

Hour, Date, Place	Summary of Events and Information	Remarks and references to Appendices
MORCOURT FEB 3. 1915.	Owing to shortage of Interpreters one withdrawn from Div¹ Train. Only 3 interpreters now allotted. Special Train order published to ensure that Supply wagons after refilling in afternoon park beside with Train Company. — This order prevents any unit sending a regimental wagon to draw Supplies. Things to notice these Units who have not sufficient capacity in the Train wagons allotted to them to draw Supplies. Visited XII Corps H.Q. re S.S.O.'s meeting. Had meeting of S.O.'s at 6.30 p.m.	

WAR DIARY
or
INTELLIGENCE SUMMARY

(Erase heading not required.)

Army Form C. 2118.

Hour, Date, Place	Summary of Events and Information	Remarks and references to Appendices
MORCOURT Dec 4. 1915	Iron rations made up.	
Dec 5. 1915.	Special order published by Division regarding Iron rations N° 420. When in future makes it necessary for units to demand iron rations to Div HQrs stating cause of demand. 2 R.O.'s detailed to make reconnaissance. Area to find quantities of straw available. Meeting of S.O.'s & R.O.'s to discuss free for coming winter.	
Dec 6. 1915	Special order published by Train HQrs making it necessary for Requisitioning Officer to inform S.S.O. the amount of money paid in hand end of each month.	F.K.

Army Form C. 2118.

WAR DIARY
or
INTELLIGENCE SUMMARY
(Erase heading not required.)

Hour, Date, Place	Summary of Events and Information	Remarks and references to Appendices
MORCOURT Oct. 7. 1915	Visits H.Qrs 3rd Army for conference re fuel supplies for coming winter — no wood available in quantity in 29 Div area. No supplies of charcoal.	Very misty early morning. Gen.
Oct. 8. 1915.	General conf. at railhead dump at LONGPRE.	Dull day - bright intervals. Warmer.
Oct. 9. 1915.	First intimation received from MTS Qmly Verbally that Divn Inf Brigades was to exchange temporarily with 67th Inf Brigade.	
Oct. 10. 1915.	Operation orders issued regarding exchange of 67th & 82nd Inf Brigade - arrangements for supplies carried out at once.	Dull morning some higher afternoon. J.76

Army Form C. 2118.

WAR DIARY
or
INTELLIGENCE SUMMARY

(Erase heading not required.)

Instructions regarding War Diaries and Intelligence Summaries are contained in F. S. Regs., Part II. and the Staff Manual respectively. Title pages will be prepared in manuscript.

Hour, Date, Place	Summary of Events and Information	Remarks and references to Appendices
MORCOURT. Oct 11. 1915.	All units of {82nd Inf Bde {27 Division} Interchanged with 67th Inf Bde continued to refill in 27th Div! area held move be completed on Oct 13. 1915. On Oct 13. 189 Coy R.S.C. (67 Inf Bde) arrived in 27 Div Area and 98 Coy R.S.C. (82 Inf Bde) moved to 22nd Div Area. There are below are effected on units shown. Oct 11. 2nd R. Irish Fusiliers } moved to 2nd D of Cornwalls L. Inf } 22nd Div Area Oct 12. 1st Leinster Regt Oct 13. 1st R. Irish Regt Hd Qrs 82 Inf Bde 98 Company R.S.C. Oct 11. 8 F. J. Welsh Fusiliers } entered 27 Div 11th Welsh Regt } area from Oct 12. } 22 Division Royal Welsh Fusiliers Oct 13. 7th S.W. also Borderers Hd Qrs 67 Bde 189 Comp? R.S.C.	Fine high weather.

J.J.C.

WAR DIARY
or
INTELLIGENCE SUMMARY
(Erase heading not required.)

Army Form C. 2118.

Hour, Date, Place	Summary of Events and Information	Remarks and references to Appendices
MONCOURT Oct. 10. 1915.	T/Lt. P.S. CARDEN A.S.C. 96 Coy A.S.C. allotted to Command 96 Coy A.S.C. vice T/Capt. H.H. RIDDLE. T/Capt. H.H. RIDDLE A.S.C. 96 Coy A.S.C. allotted to Command 98 Coy A.S.C. vice T/Lt. P.S. CARDEN.	
Oct. 11. 1915.	Following allotment of officers made in 27 Div Train T/S/Lt. R.D. DAVIES A.S.C. from 96 Coy A.S.C. to 98 Coy A.S.C. T/S/Lt. G.E. YOUNG A.S.C. from 98 Coy A.S.C. to 96 Coy A.S.C.	
Oct. 12. 1915.	—	Fine bright weather
Oct. 13. 1915.	Visited WIENCOURT HdQrs 22 Div Train to discuss with O.C. Train various points regarding transfer of 189 & 98 Coy R.S.C. Circular Memo Q/111/4 issued by 27 Div calling attention to greater need of A.S.C. units Supervising their First Line Transport	J.S.C.

Army Form C. 2118.

WAR DIARY
or
INTELLIGENCE SUMMARY

(Erase heading not required.)

Instructions regarding War Diaries and Intelligence Summaries are contained in F. S. Regs., Part II, and the Staff Manual respectively. Title pages will be prepared in manuscript.

Hour, Date, Place	Summary of Events and Information	Remarks and references to Appendices
MORCOURT		
Dec 14. 1915.	Visited AMIENS re certain possibility of obtaining "Anthracite" Smithy Coal.	
Dec 14. 1915.	12th Corps under Q703 gave authority for S.O's to issue petrol in exchange to French authorities (repairing loads with petrol-driven vehicles) if required.	
Dec 15. 1915	Fourth HQrs 3rd Army (DDST 17.) to draw rations extras for 27 Div (Quick lime Smiths Coal)	
Dec 16. 1915	Refitting for all units 27 Div allowed to 3.30am. That 4 h.w. 10th Labour Battalion arrived in 27 Div Area Now billetted at LE HAMEL.	F.T.G

Army Form C. 2118.

WAR DIARY
or
INTELLIGENCE SUMMARY

(Erase heading not required.)

Instructions regarding War Diaries and Intelligence Summaries are contained in F. S. Regs., Part II. and the Staff Manual respectively. Title pages will be prepared in manuscript.

Hour, Date, Place	Summary of Events and Information	Remarks and references to Appendices
MORCOURT		
Oct 17. 1915.	Visited Corps (XII) HQ to report on Supplies generally to A.Q.M.G.	
Oct 18. 1915.	MAJOR E.H. COLLEN D.S.O. DAA & QMG 27 Div left for 12 Div being appointed AA rank to that Division.	
	20th Heavy Battery arrived in 27 Divl Area from Villers in LE MANEL.	
Oct 19. 1915.		
Oct 20. 1915.	Information received that 67th Brigade would rejoin 22nd Division and 82nd Bde 27 Division.	

Army Form C. 2118.

WAR DIARY
or
INTELLIGENCE SUMMARY
(Erase heading not required.)

Instructions regarding War Diaries and Intelligence Summaries are contained in F. S. Regs., Part II. and the Staff Manual respectively. Title pages will be prepared in manuscript.

Hour, Date, Place	Summary of Events and Information	Remarks and references to Appendices
MORCOURT Oct 21 1915	189 Coy A.S.C. 67 Inf Bde reported 27 Div 98 Coy A.S.C. 82 " " " 27 Div. Battalions of 22nd Div attached 27 Div moved out of 27 Div area, to rejoin their own division. Indermedlowen units left 27 Div. These taken on for purpose of feeding by Division as stated — All units left 27 Div with supply wagons loaded with supplies for consumption 22 OCt A Coy 7th Lehr Battalion taken on by A.S.O. 26 Div. 10th Lehr Battalion " " " " " 137 A Troops Coy R.E. " " " 12th Corps Troops S Col 183 Dismounting Coy R.E. " " " S.S.O. 26 Div 20 Heavy Battery Rly A. " " " 12th Corps Troops S Col Approved by [signature] J.C.	—

[signature]

Army Form C. 2118.

WAR DIARY
or
INTELLIGENCE SUMMARY
(Erase heading not required.)

Hour, Date, Place	Summary of Events and Information	Remarks and references to Appendices
MORCOURT. Oct 22. 1915.	2 Canadian Heavy Bty taken over by 1 Corps Troops. J. Gunn for rationing. Ref. TRANSPORT "The following official order issued by Division. They are to marched as to separate parts in order to avoid shortening the Heavy draught horses or to horses in the same column. they are to be marched at the head of it." Light draught horses are not to be hooked in front of Heavy Draught horses." 2nd Army Sup. Col. reported 27 Div. preparatory to troops of 6th French Army relieving 27 Division	7.76

Army Form C. 2118.

WAR DIARY
or
INTELLIGENCE SUMMARY
(Erase heading not required.)

Hour, Date, Place	Summary of Events and Information	Remarks and references to Appendices
MORCOURT. Mch 23.1915	Ass'y Germany Hd + Div'l Cyclists moved to PONT-DE-METZ 19th Bde R.F.A. - - BOVES. No. 16 Mobile Vet - - BOVES Div'l Amm Col - - BOVES. In order to resume to normal system of drawing supplies in the field there was no refilling of Train Vehicles on this day. Supply Column drew at railhead 23rd with supplies for today 24th and packed loaded night of 23/24th. 82 Sqt Res 82 Sub Amm 1st heavy R.G. 129 Howitzer R.F.A. + 186 Coy A.S.C. moved by march route to BOVES Div'l Transport units mentioned above Mch 23. moving neighbourhood of AILLY SUR SOMME	J 26
Mch 24. 1915		

WAR DIARY
of
INTELLIGENCE SUMMARY

(Erase heading not required.)

Army Form C. 2118.

Instructions regarding War Diaries and Intelligence Summaries are contained in F. S. Regs., Part II. and the Staff Manual respectively. Title pages will be prepared in manuscript.

Hour, Date, Place	Summary of Events and Information	Remarks and references to Appendices
MORCOURT Mar 27. 1915	Refilling of 80th Bde formation took place at MORCOURT 9am. 81st Bde formation CERISY at 9am. 82 Bde formation at BOVES at 4pm. Supply wagons of 82nd Bde formation proceeded empty with 98 Coy ASC from CERISY to BOVES refilling at BOVES on arrival there. D.Troops formation less those otherwise notified refilled at MORCOURT 9am. On Mar 26, North West 19th RFA (Horse) BOVES at 9am. Supply wagons accompanied units in move forward for BOVES & AILLY-SUR-SOMME neighbourhood Divl. Cyclists & Divl. Yeomanry were refilled at PONT de METZ at 11am.	✠JC

Army Form C. 2118.

WAR DIARY
or
INTELLIGENCE SUMMARY

(Erase heading not required.)

Hour, Date, Place	Summary of Events and Information	Remarks and references to Appendices
MORCOURT Oct 25 1915	95 Coy A.S.C. 7th Div'n Train moved by march route to BOVES, bivouacking there night of 25/26 proceeding to BOVELLES on morning of Oct 26. 80th Bde Formation arrived MERICOURT 9 a.m. 81st " " CERISY 9 a.m. 82nd " " FERRIERES 3.30 p.m. Divn Bde Formation moved to hospital billets in neighbourhood of FERRIERES from BOVES on morning of Oct 25. Supply wagons moved from BOVES with 95 Coy A.S.C. empty returning on arrival at FERRIERES with supplies for consumption on 26. D.T.'s formation (less units otherwise mentioned) refilled at BOVES on arrival of supply wagons which moved with 95 Coy A.S.C. empty from MORCOURT.	F.G.

WAR DIARY
or
INTELLIGENCE SUMMARY
(Erase heading not required.)

Army Form C. 2118.

Hour, Date, Place	Summary of Events and Information	Remarks and references to Appendices
BOVELLES Dec 20. 1915.	81st Bde formation moved from WARFUSEE ABANCOURT to BOVES. 80th Bde formation moved from Rendu line area to neighbourhood of CERISY 82nd Bde formation moved from neighbourhood of FERRIERES to neighbourhood of FRESNOY AU VAL Refilling took place as follows:- 81st Bde formation BOVES 4 p.m. (Supply wagons of this formation moved empty late 97 Coy A.S.C. on march route from CERISY to BOVES refilling as stated on arrival at dump area. 82nd Bde formation BOVELLES 10 a.m. ATC Supply wagons of this formation moved loaded with 98 Coy A.S.C. by march route to BOVES & FRESNOY. Supplies were then dumped with units and the wagons returned to 98 Coy A.S.C.'s near FRICAMPS.	[signature]

WAR DIARY
or
INTELLIGENCE SUMMARY

(Erase heading not required.)

Army Form C. 2118.

Hour, Date, Place	Summary of Events and Information	Remarks and references to Appendices
BOVELLES. Oct 26. 1915.	80th Bde formation arrived at CERISY 10am. D.Troops formation arrived at BOVELLES 3pm. Supply wagons of units moved into 9 & 6 by A.S.C. from bivouac at BOVES rejoining on arrival at BOVELLES. Item proceeding to these units, carrying supplies for consumption on 27.10.15.	
Oct 27. 1915.	Railhead changed from VILLERS-BRETONNEUX to AILLY-SUR-SOMME. 80th Inf.Bde formation moved throughout of BOVES and bivouaced at that place north of 27/28/15. Refilling took place at BOVES 3pm. Supply wagons of units accompanying 96 by A.S.C. unitely refining on arrival of that unit in BOVES.	J.76

Army Form C. 2118.

WAR DIARY
or
INTELLIGENCE SUMMARY

(Erase heading not required.)

Instructions regarding War Diaries and Intelligence Summaries are contained in F. S. Regs., Part II. and the Staff Manual respectively. Title pages will be prepared in manuscript.

Hour, Date, Place	Summary of Events and Information	Remarks and references to Appendices
BOVELLES. Oct 27. 1915.	81st Bde formation arrived at BOVELLES. 3pm. en route march from BOVES to new area neighbourhood of FLORICOURT. 47 Coy M.T. moved with Bricks to FLORICOURT. 82nd Bde formation arrived at FRESNOY. 10am — arrived at BOVELLES. 10am Div. Troops "	
Oct 28. 1915.	80th Bde formation moved to new area neighbourhood of FERRIERES refusing at their place en route there at 8pm. 96 Coy A.S.C. moved from BOVES with supply wagons of units 80th Bde formation empty refusing at FERRIERES when conveying rations & mails wagons returning to 96 Coy A.S.C. after dumping.	F.J.G

WAR DIARY
or
INTELLIGENCE SUMMARY
(Erase heading not required.)

Army Form C. 2118.

Hour, Date, Place	Summary of Events and Information	Remarks and references to Appendices
BOVELLES		
Dec 28. 1915	81st Bde formation arrived at FLORENCOURT 10 a.m. 9th Bde formation arrived at FRESNOY 10 a.m. Divl. Troops formation — — BOVELLES 10 a.m.	
Dec 29. 1915	Refittings normally resumed this day and will move to rest area completed.	All day
Dec 30. 1915	Reported to A.D.S.T. 3rd Army supply services generally satisfactory.	All day
Dec 31. 1915	Handed over 27 Bn Cord stores reserve at CERISY-GAILLY to S.S.O. 5th Division.	Can held ray.

Smith Major
Mark Franco
F.S.C.
D 31st

121/7637

27th June 1941

Ivar Strand.
Storøen 10   24/11 Divisionai Strani.

November 1915

WAR DIARY
or
INTELLIGENCE SUMMARY
(Erase heading not required.)

Army Form C. 2118

Place	Date	Hour	Summary of Events and Information	Remarks and references to Appendices
BOVELLES	Nov 3rd 1915		First intimation received that 27th Division had been ordered to prepare for leaving France for the East, with the exception of 27th Divisional Supply Column and the majority of the 27th Divisional Train. The following ASC details to accompany the Division:— S.S.O. All Supply & Requisitioning Officers 1 Transport Officer from H.Q. Company 1 Sub: from each of 3 Oat Companies 1 " " above officer All Batmen of Supply details T/Capt. F. H. Wright 93 Company took over command of	

Army Form C. 2118

WAR DIARY
or
INTELLIGENCE SUMMARY

(Erase heading not required.)

Instructions regarding War Diaries and Intelligence Summaries are contained in F. S. Regs., Part II. and the Staff Manual respectively. Title Pages will be prepared in manuscript.

Place	Date	Hour	Summary of Events and Information	Remarks and references to Appendices
BOVELLES	Nov 3rd 1915		96 Company vice T/Capt H.H. Riddle T/Capt H.H. Riddle transferred to 95 (H.Q.) Company A.S.C. as second in command.	
	Nov 9th		Lieut. A. Boulton A.S.C. transferred from 95 (H.Q.) Coy to 96 Company vice	
	Nov 13th		Capt. W.D. Anderton R.A.M.C. attached to the train as M.O. transferred to 21st Field Ambulance for duty. Lieut. R.H. Alabaster R.A.M.C. joined 29th Divisional Train as M.O. vice Capt. W.D. Anderton.	

Army Form C. 2118

WAR DIARY
or
INTELLIGENCE SUMMARY
(Erase heading not required.)

Instructions regarding War Diaries and Intelligence Summaries are contained in F.S. Regs., Part II. and the Staff Manual respectively. Title Pages will be prepared in manuscript.

Place	Date	Hour	Summary of Events and Information	Remarks and references to Appendices
BOVELLES	Nov. 12th 1915		The undermentioned Officers detailed for attachments for duty as follows:— Lieut. O. Boulter 26 Cy attd to 83rd & 2nd Stat. T/2 Lieut C.L. Richardson 7tCy " to 81st T/2 & attd T/2 Lieut A.D. Davies 95tCy " to 89tT/2 attd	
	Nov 12-14th		During the days Nov 12th to 14th 1915 inclusive the Train received over 2650 horses and mules, to convert and exchange with the various units of the Divison, prior to the Establishment of the Divison being altered to comply with the Special Establishment of Salonika Force S.w.2 dated 4/11/15.	

1875. Wt. W593/826 1,000,000 4/15 J.B.C. & A. A.D.S.S./Forms/C. 2118.

WAR DIARY
or
INTELLIGENCE SUMMARY
(Erase heading not required.)

Army Form C. 2118

Instructions regarding War Diaries and Intelligence Summaries are contained in F.S. Regs., Part II. and the Staff Manual respectively. Title Pages will be prepared in manuscript.

Place	Date	Hour	Summary of Events and Information	Remarks and references to Appendices
BOVELLES	October 10th-14th		Time being & exchanging of horses & Mules was received out very satisfactorily.	This being & Mules was not all 5 days
	Nov. 15th		S.S.O. Left with advance guard for MARSEILLES	
	Nov. 16th	So 4 Inf Bde entrained at LONGEAU and left for MARSEILLES, all horses 1st line transport of the Bde attached to 96 Company A.S.C. and remained at FERRIERES. Orders received that 20 other Officers under 25 years of age to proceed with Division. 5th Inf. B.de moved its billets vacated by 4th Bde. 97 Company A.S.C. moved to new billets at FERRIERES	

Army Form C. 2118

WAR DIARY
or
INTELLIGENCE SUMMARY
(Erase heading not required.)

Instructions regarding War Diaries and Intelligence Summaries are contained in F.S. Regs., Part II and the Staff Manual respectively. Title Pages will be prepared in manuscript.

Place	Date	Hour	Summary of Events and Information	Remarks and references to Appendices
BOVELLES	November 20th		Major E. Latham admitted to hospital.	
	Nov. 21st		Their R.B. Pargo-Lyffe admitted to hospital. 1st line Transport of Co. B ex. left by rail for LONGEAU Staba.	
	Nov. 23rd		1/Lieut T.D. Collen & Supply Details of No. Company accompanied 2nd Inf. Bde Transport, & Lieut W.A. Leggat reported for duty, & posted to 98 Company as R.O. 82nd Bde. 96 Company a.S.C. moved for FERRIERES & new billets SAISSEVAL	

WAR DIARY
or
INTELLIGENCE SUMMARY

(Erase heading not required.)

Army Form C. 2118

Instructions regarding War Diaries and Intelligence Summaries are contained in F. S. Regs., Part II and the Staff Manual respectively. Title Pages will be prepared in manuscript.

Place	Date	Hour	Summary of Events and Information	Remarks and references to Appendices
BOUELLES	Nov. 24th		98 Company HQ. moved from FRICAMPS to BOUELLES in FERRIERS.	
			8½ Sec. of 98 & part of 892nd Inf. Bt. (both O.R.s two hungry) returned at LONGEAU & left by rail.	
	Nov. 25.		Remainder of 892nd Inf. Bt. left Sept by rail. 7 Lieut Taylor & 719th Lieut Griffith went supply.	
			Details of 98 Co. 982nd Inf. Co. accompanied Transport	
			7 82nd G.C.	
			7/Lt. Stones and Lieut Leggatt and Lefty details of 98 Company Co. accompanied Transport of 982 Bt.	
			Lieut R.C. Kelly on rebuild for duty & joined as Transport Sub. to 98 Company C.S.C.	

Army Form C. 2118

WAR DIARY
or
INTELLIGENCE SUMMARY
(Erase heading not required.)

Instructions regarding War Diaries and Intelligence Summaries are contained in F. S. Regs., Part II. and the Staff Manual respectively. Title Pages will be prepared in manuscript.

Place	Date	Hour	Summary of Events and Information	Remarks and references to Appendices
BOVELLES	Nov 26"		2/Lieut T. R. Low reported for at. G & Duties as transfer. Lieut. to 98 Coy A.K.C.	
	Nov 27"		Lt. Col. A. R. Liddell C.O. 9th Divl. Train granted Lv. & 1st Div. C.A. Capt. C. G. Seller assumed Temp. Command of Train.	

A.H.C.Ashen
Lieut. + A.C.

www.ingramcontent.com/pod-product-compliance
Lightning Source LLC
Chambersburg PA
CBHW081550160426
43191CB00011B/1883